A
Poetry Archive

Volume 6
Lizards, Way Poems and Gariwerd
2014–2016

Frank Prem

Wild Arancini Press
2025

Publication Details

Title: A Poetry Archive Volume 6:
  Lizards, Way Poems and Gariwerd 2014–2016

ISBN: 978-1-923166-37-0 (p-bk)
ISBN: 978-1-923166-38-7 (e-bk))

Published by Wild Arancini Press
Copyright © 2025 Frank Prem
All rights reserved:

No part of this publication may be reproduced, stored in a retrieval system, or transmitted in any form or by any means, electronic, mechanical, photocopying, recording or otherwise, without prior written permission from the publisher and author.
A catalogue record for this book is available from the National Library of Australia.

Cover Image: Wild Arancini Press

It is always a good time to learn a new language

CONTENTS

A Poetry Archive Volume 6

2014	3
2015 (1)	39
2015 (2)	63
2015 (3)	97
2016 (1)	127
2016 (2)	155
Listening to Gariwerd	171
A Blue-Tongued Lizard Life	187
More Lizards	231
Way Poems	243
After Words	283
Index of Poems	285
Author Information	291
What Readers Say	295

A Poetry Archive Volume 6

Introduction

The *A Poetry Archive* series captures the great majority of poetic work undertaken by Frank Prem and not published in dedicated collections elsewhere.

The current collection (*Volume 6*) continues the reorientation of Prem's writing to a more direct communication with the reader. A more conversational tone that has become characteristic of his later work.

Volume 6 captures work undertaken during 2014–2016, and further develops his distinctive poetic voice, including a fascination with Blue-Tongued Skinks and other backyard lizards, contemplations of The Way, and the stunning impact of a visit to Gariwerd.

Each poem a universe, complete.

2014

mind so

> *ah*
> *ahahah*
> *ah*

a breeze soughs
through my mind
riffling cicadas and crickets
that chirp
and chirrup
through every absence of thought
and vacant moment

> *ahahah*

I
am ruffled

the concept of . . .

the concept of *vengeance*
being a troubled field . . .

I find that I am
self-bound up in a restless —
mid-night waking —
conscience

wishing I was a better man
while praying
little prayers
beneath my breath
for the targeted visitation
of a typhoon
or a heart attack

2014

indigo u

hue and me
we'll fly beneath the rainbow
in between the violet
and the blue

we'll dance along the sunrays
to the raindrops

hold my hand
and we will become
the rainbow

in circles

I walk an old dog
on a lead in case she wanders

she is blind and gets lost

sometimes it makes me wonder
how much longer
will I walk an old dog on a lead
around in circles on a lead
around in circles
on a lead

she's been a good dog
we've grown old together
sometimes I have to wonder
who led who

but she's a good dog
with bad legs
and no eyes
who still likes to walk around in circles
on a lead
where she's safe just in case
she might wander

shadow

wheel my shadow home
at the end of the night
it is climbing walls
without me

it glides across cobbled walks
slips beneath my heels
makes a face behind my back
then runs up and down
on trees
and the walls of houses
that I pass by

drag my shadow home
it has no license
to attend wild parties
without me

and I feel
it is having a good time
and drinking
more than I should

saying things
that I'd rather keep close

slinking in and out
of the darker corners
of my mind
and into my mouth

saying things
I should not say

the locale

Wooragee is a ten kid school
on the road between two towns
Leneva is another stop
on that line

Glenrowan is a tourist dump
that once held up a town
it's got the petrol bowser
on the freeway outside of Wangaratta

Chiltern hosts an antiques store
Rutherglen is growing grapes
and a crawl between her wineries
will *dis-com-bob* and *un-array* you

Beechworth was a loony bin
and a prison until they slammed their doors
now it's a nest of shopkeepers
and the festivals that make their tills sing

    ring-a-ding

that make my mind go

    ding-a-ling

and I'm up here in Stanley
among the wanna-be bourgeoisie
who are all trying to make their latte
out of a tree-change

a study in meteorology

I watch the rain
I count each drop
then write it in my journal

day after day
each drop adds up
in the end I'll swim a year

I count the rain
I watch each drop
then draw it in my sketchpad

fall after fall
my book fills up
in the end I'll float tomorrow

drop by drop
drop by drop
the rain falls down

it will not falter

I watch it fall
I see it run

a river on my window

an ocean swell
in the corner of the sill

when flying

arise sir raincoat
there's a wind beneath your tether
fluff out your arms
as if
you were flying

you and your best mate
a girl-coat in mauve
at full stretch and unruffled
just like
you were flying

on a string
you might be a kite
to skip and dive
all over the sky

or
as a bag full of random air
you could dance
just as the leaves do

but you sir raincoat
are attached to a hook
and only your sail spreads
as though
you were flying

yet the wind may still raise you
up down and tail out
a superman cape in rehearsal
for when
you are flying

three echoes

i)

standing at the verge
he threw his voice
single-handed
as far across the gap
as his strength would allow

hand shading his brow
he watched
as it arced elegantly
and returned

ii)

timidly she approached
near to the edge
uncertainty radiating
then listened

straightened

she took one further pace forward
threw her arms back
and smiled

the whistle of the wind
sang her name
to the tune
of *home*

iii)

he danced in the night
on a cliff top
with nothing to say

no call

there was silence
apart from the speech of a small fire
but he needed no sound
to belong

he felt in his being
he had been heard

sharp

how sleek you magpie
how spiv your slick-back
your *only-one-chance* eyes
and *brook-no-beg-your* beak

keen is not alike
to nice

whet an answer on a sharp-stone
to every debt then
direct your bill

a fall of finches

they descend like spent leaves
yellow and brown and red

a wafted flutter
from branch to ground
as though a zephyr
whispered a wish
and the thought gave breath
to the deed

in a murmur of suggestion
the illusion of stillness
shivers

to hop and peck
and skitter
as a rustled animation
of winter

author, author

I've never owned a pocket sized pistol
but I'll pull my six-gun out
with no hesitation

    blam!

    blam!

you better stay on the right side of me
I can be a dangerous man
~

I don't go much for ships or boats
but with a patch to cover my eye
I'll cruise the high seas

    arrh!

    arrh!

if I see your sail
from the top of my wave
I will tack you down
~

I'm no great shakes for wild romance
but with a rose between my teeth
I'll dance flamenco

    ra-ta-ta!

you can clack the castanets
while I stamp around you

~

I don't get out much
from behind my desk
but . . .

I can see *myself* at *your* place
opening a bottle

    POP!

if I can call your lips
into a picture
in my mind
I'll pen you into this story

2014

an uncertainty in silver

I grow old now
in the ways that a man *must* grow old

the aching of the spine
the weakening of the eyes
and the slow-down
that happens each morning
and again in the night

it is harder to stand up
as tall as I was once
in the prime of my youth

who would have thought this could happen
to a man with the world to set right
and a million and one tasks to do
before supper every day

between one rub of the eyes
and the next
reading glasses have appeared
and there is slightly less hair
though slightly *more* silver
an encroaching bewilderment
at the youth of today
and a certain sure knowledge
that the world is too strange
to endure

angling the big deep

I will entice you with lines
I have baited and burley-ed
cast with my strength to the sea
in which words filled with elegant meaning
swim by in phrases that turn
and twist
on a wave danced in undertones
then left near-expired on my beach
by a receding tide

I will talk my fish
to land . . .

you
drawn by a lure
and the romance of angling a moon
risen up with the sun down
so full and so warm as she shines me
in ripples and stanzas that break on near rhymes
from far off by the horizon
all the way in
to a splash on your toes

I am thinking in small tugs and nibbles
experiencing occasional bites

the big deep is thrashing
just under the surface
not quite within grasp
but perhaps it will come if I call . . .

perhaps it will come
if *you* call

2014

Ned's Bakery (Beechworth)

the Beechworth Bakery specialises
in Ned Kelly

bushranger sandwiches
kelly country pies
and bee sting custard discount rewards
for any information
and just five cents

old Ned went on the lam
but they caught him
and I am seated behind a corner
yet Marie strolls over with my coffee
says
I found you
and she did

this is the kind of place
old men wear their akubra's inside
no need to remove them

they could hang a pistol
on the outside of their pants
to turn the scene *olde timey*
like the shops outside the window
that look a hundred years ago

people on the street are sniffing
for their whiff of him
but Ned Kelly isn't here any more
just a focaccia and a bakery bear
in a fluffy hat

Frank Prem

lament for a lost _uzz (1)

I have loved the smell of flowers
the nectar taste of ripened fruit
an apple
a pear
straw_erries with cream

_uttery canola
spread on pumpkin-_read toast
then _reakfast yellow-_ox
or leatherwood honey
dripped slowly
from my knife onto the _read

the mead cakes my grandma _aked
were to expire for
and vanilla
my favourite ice-cream
in a cone

where have they gone
these simple _eauties

what has happened
to change the world
to shades of _rown and grey

I wish I'd started a hive
_ack when a little more
might have _een
a lot

lament for a lost _uzz (2)

the eucalypt still puts out _lossoms

we chose it for the flowers
and planted it where sun
would highlight the crimson
and we could see it
during morning coffee

and watch the _irds
_usy in their days

I see the honeyeaters
and other flying creatures
_ut they work silently now
where once upon a time
it was a _uzz

and yes
the tree still shows itself
in _lossom
_ut there was less to see last year
and there is less again this year

I wonder
if next year
will _e the same

prrrty

it's the spiney-bill show
they're here and there
they're everywhere
farting their wings
through the sky

prrrty prrrt they rise
from shrub to tree
prrrty prrrt prrrt prrrt

who'd have thought the troupe
were so many

I'd only seen them
in their one's and two's
but they are lined up now
like a well drilled cast
when the show goes on

they're set to fly

buzzy buzz buzz buzz
the bees applaud them
from the chandelier tree

prrrrty prrrt prrrt prrrt

buzzy buzz buzz

the show may be over
but the wings fart on

there again (the corri-dog)

the corri-dog is there again

when I turn to leave the bedroom
she wasn't there when I looked before
but an old blind dog has to know her tricks
and if there's something happening
she needs to be where . . .

the corri-dog is there again

this passageway was completely clear
just a moment ago
yet she looks so innocent sleeping
as though a long-time fixture
like a pattern laid into the carpet or . . .

the corri-dog who is there again

I almost trod her tail
and she looks at me dull-eyed
like a sentry doing her duty
then sprawls asleep
just where the traffic mostly passes

the corri-dog

uke-latin (olé)

I wish I could play the ukulele
but my finger gets stuck on C
if only I could play the strings more gaily
what a fine ukulelist I would be

but I strum strum strum
and it sounds so glum
because up and down is all
that I can do
yet if I did a strumming pattern
I could make it sound quite latin
señorita I would play it for you

and so I wish that I could play the ukulele
maybe progress as far as G
a chord that needs to use three fingers
and which is two more than a C

then I could strum strum strum
a two chord song
though up and down is all
that I can do
I might find a strumming pattern
that would make me sound quite latin
señorita I could play my song for you

yes señorita
I would play my song for you
olé!

wattle and heart

I have watched them
the wattlebird family
as many as ten
in an unruly mob
worrying the waratah
pouncing upon the centre
of a deep crimson bloom
beak and tongue plunged deep
into the nectar

until displaced
by yet another of this vast extended family
of bouncing bullying buffoons

on the flight path
from the gum trees across the road
they zero in
as though each were a dart
cast by a steady hand
aimed bull's-eye
at my heart
before veering away one degree
two
to alight on the crimson

>   *bounce*

>   *bounce*

these birds are not small

>   *bounce*

and when they leave
they depart from the same runway
into the eucalypt forest
for other desirable lickings

but this one . . .

this one is young
and the path not as straight
as it seems

he has luffed to the left
and not stayed true
collided almost
into my arm
then veered away sharp-ish
more disturbed at the error
than I at our confrontation

corrected
then gone

this wattlebird family
is large
unruly and loud
and cause a smile
when the young stray
slightly
and almost touch my heart

above and below

the wind sings aloud an unquiet song
a eucalypt bows its branches
the rustle of the grass is eager to tell secrets
that it shares in a hushed murmur

flutter leaves

twirl and turn you dancers

confound my eyes
with your green sequined sway
I could be mesmerized
among your kisses

oh wind
you sing an unquiet song
crying above the eucalypts
while the rustling grass reveals nothing at all

all I hear is the whisper

but these green young leaves
are dancing
my eyes pursue each sequined sway
flutter once again

I could die
in a kiss so sweet

two insect asides

the movement I saw
from the corner of my eye
was a black-spotted white-winged
cabbage butterfly

it flew lazy above
the red-flower bed
fluttered toward pink
then went mauve instead

~

the bees on the bottlebrush
are in a love affair
erotically they're rubbing
sticky stamens everywhere

but like any common drunkard
it's staggering to see
an infatuated fool release
a spray of boozed-bee wee

anchor

my thoughts today are spider webs
threads and filament
delicately held at origin
and destination

they glisten in the light
sway with every current breeze

they are my way to there
and back again

my anchor

mopoke

I will listen to the mopoke's song
hoot me gentle
toward the deep

for a day is done
and the darkness come
to enfold my dreams
and me
to keep

    mopoke
    mopoke

hoot me now
to sleep

2014

for my help

did your father talk to you about
the fading of his strength
when he passed into his eighties

I remember him as a quiet man
perched upon a stool
who sometimes gave a thoughtful gift
that showed he really knew
what went on
around him

I recall he seemed to lose his wind
he seemed to lose
the vitality that keeps a man
alive and somehow moving

and *you* are in your eighties now
the wind has long since fled
from out your sails
though you keep on working hard
to keep on working hard
and up till now that's been enough

but here you are and asking

and I wondered did your father
ask you too
was that the *why* of all those hours
you took his toil upon your shoulders
and is *that* why you and I
are talking now

to my mind

the air is still
thunder rolling
a leaf twirls from the tree
spins to the ground

the twittering of birds
surrounds me
calling life
before the storm

in this light
all is beautiful

I think of you

the air has me suspended
in a moment
between the boom of drum rolls
that climb through me
up from my feet

I am held beneath
loose strands of floating grey
luminescent in a light
that envelops me
with a hint of rain
played gently
through a ruff of waving leaves

that bring *you*
to my mind

state of min . . . (gee-up)

gee-up

this is how I drive mysel . . .

gee-up

this is how I force another lin . . .

gee-up

it's just another form of motivatio . . .

gee-up

when I can't write for far too lon . . .

gee-up – come on just put the pen on pape . . .
gee-up – try thinking less try writing mor . . .
gee-up – get along get along get along and scribin . . .
gee-up – the whole world wants to hear another poe . . .

there's a new rhythm in my felt-ti . . .

gee-up

I feel it flowing like a son . . .

gee-up

how could I have thought that I was dryin . . .

gee-up

this writing's just a state of min . . .

yes it seems
it's just a state of mine

sweet dream

with her face in the sun
her skin seems aglow
her eyes creep slowly closed
and the book in her hands
slips a little lower

there is a glitter in the air
like mead conjured from honey
the warm I can feel
is a sea made from the gold
she floats in

and the birdcall she hears
is the honeyeater's song
the buzz in her mind —
like the drone note of slumber —
is the hum at the heart of a bee

today in the sun
with her eyes closed tight
it's a butterfly that stirs the breeze
and the effect is to call
a sweet dream

2015 (1)

my girl (the mantis)

my girl is angry
she looks as if she'll bite me
if I don't please her

her eyes are pinpoint
I don't know
what I've done
to raise her ire

my girl is hungry
I look at her in lust
she says she'll eat me

I adore her
can't stop myself
from making passes

from
making love

for when she nips me
I arouse
and if she bites
I can go
for hours
my femme fatale
I can't resist her
or
I will die

my girl's so sexy
a shimmy with her thorax
mesmerizes

when she holds me
arms that keep me still
take me
to her mandibles
of love

my girl is watching
she has me in her gaze
and there's no leaving

I love her kisses
at my neck
I'm so in love
I've lost my mind

cockatoo committee

the cocky's council is in session
on the lawn

the chair-bird
is high-stepping
around the gathering
hoiking scaly legs
and pristine pantaloons
as though to avoid
an unpleasant issue
left over from the last item
that was moved

a sulphur crest is raised
to make a point of order
white heads
bob up and down
as they confer

a creak
follows a croak
and soon a screeching
leads to
the biscuit break and then
a cup of *cha*

when reconvened
there's sure to be
some dancing
led by the old rocker
Poll
for a bit of scratch

the session will be closed
at the end of business
or when the lawn
is all chopped up—
whichever's first

then they'll all be off
for parts unknown
their goodbye's screaming
to bring the minutes and decisions
of this vital and important meeting
to the impatient
waiting ears
in the snow-white flock

the girl who had her red shoes on

she danced across the floor with her red shoes on
clicked her heels in the air with her red shoes on
she leapt between the leaves with her red shoes on
until she stood right at the top of the tree

then she tripped across the sky with her red shoes on
and gambolled among the clouds with her red shoes on
she flew abreast the breeze with her red shoes on
until she'd blown all the way around the world

she circled the sun with her red shoes on
swung between the stars with her red shoes on
she left a yellow trail with her red shoes on
then she stopped to have a rest upon the moon

rain-song

we are waiting for the rain
smell the fire in the air

> *thunder growls a warning*
> *lightning sets the spark*

we are waiting for the fire
search the air for rain

> *thunder prowls beyond the smoke*
> *lightning splits the dark*

and here it comes
rain is slanting down

> *here it comes*
> *the roof is a raindrop sound*

there it goes
let it fall and fall again

> *yes it goes*
> *like it's never going to end*

sky rupture

the sky is a ruptured fury
of anger
strobe and growl
poor humour of the belly
diarrhea
constipation

it's cracked the shits
that's all I know

a sun-burnt trilling

I heard an old girl on the radio
sing/speaking the 'sun-burnt country' poem
accompanied by a slow-poke piano

quavery
not quite spoken-word
not quite a song
almost a trill in the words

and I wondered
how dorothea
would have heard it

very local knowledge

how did I know that *Gary*
referred to *Indiana*
the two words were separated
by a page

I guess I've grown up
with so much *Americana*
that I almost know
where every town is
and every whistle stop
what *WA* and *AZ*
and *NY* mean

guess I know where
almost everything
in *America* is

but does anyone know that I live
in *Stanley*
or that *Murmungee*
is just a short drive
down *The Gap*

and what about
where *Whorouly*
and *Milawa*
or *Myrtleford* are
if not right here
where I can touch them

but I don't suppose
anyone but me

either knows or cares
about *Chiltern*
or *Wooragee*

and why would they
when the local heroes
myths and legends
don't travel
anywhere

huff the lights out

well here we go
old Lee-lu dog
I'll turn the light out
on your huff-ering

last night you slept
in the kitchen
tonight on your rug
in the corner of my room

and I can hear you
deep breaths and stertor wuffs
as though about to start
a shredded bark
that is all your age
has left you

turning the light out
should make no change at all
to a blind grumping dog
in my corner
but maybe there is a feeling
that suggests the night
and maybe there's an absence
when I turn it off

and maybe now
you'll stop huffing me
so both of us
can get to sleep

harsh laughter

two kookaburras sound as though
they are choking

until they get started

a harsh laugh
even so hard-earned
must be better
than a cry

my god
now there's six of them

the last mellow

last rays play a golden glow
across the eucalypts
as day fades

a little patch of mellow
lights the green
familiar as a smile
before the sombre shades
of grey descend

and the trees
come close together
as a hug to hold the warm
and to stand —
a solemn totem —
before darkness

a eucalypt embrace
before the night

the wooing of the wind

I heard the sound
of a woo-wooing wind
whisper a name to the sky

softly the murmur
first rose
then it fell
but the secret it sang
was not mine

yet the thought of that name
had nestled closely to me
beneath the shirt that I wore
near as skin

the warmth that it gave
was like a memory of you
and that sound that I'd thought
brought you close

perhaps
the name in the wind

was yours

the blackberry

blackberries sprawl
further every night
from green leaf
to tendril
to bramble
rambling briar

blackberries bite
like the avid blade
of a cross tooth saw
they grip
then they tear

bastard fruit

eagle

I'm having daydreams
about a night dream
about an eagle

and I wonder
over the meaning
that I've lost

because I well recall
the *what* it was
but I cannot place the *why*

and in the middle of the day
I've got eagles
on my mind

is it my totem . . .some symbol
for what I am
or a message
from the spirit world

> *the talon points the way*

and if I go too slow
there might be a yellow beak
at my behind

I'm having daydreams
about my night dreams
about that raptor

and I wonder . . .

> *where is the meaning*
> *I've misplaced*
>
> *is there a harpy*
> *at my shoulder*
> *spreading its wings out over me*
>
> *in the middle of the day*
> *why is this eagle*
> *on my mind*

currawong sky

these currawongs
are flying crazy

three are east
while one has turned
to go back home

their mournful notes
cry such a pity—
the need to go
the heart to stayy —

and these currawongs
are circling madly

I've heard that rain
comes close behind
their call

they fill the sky
with darkness turning
goodbye the light

an evening falls

shadow dancing

the shadow
by the streetlamp's shine
grows longer

it thins
then it stretches out
like a pointer
to the dark

running ahead
or behind me the shadow
whispers conversations
away from any where
I stand

how can I know
all the things my shadow does
with its elongated head
that reaches away
into the night

how can I feel
all the things my shadow feels
flattened on the pavement
no body yielding
to my touch

so
I think that I must dance
with my shadow
pretend I am holding
while it pretends
it is holding

we will short-step ourselves
around and around
the lamppost

in a no-dance of any substance
approaching a sort of one-ness
that is nothing but a movement
in a transparency of colour
that is dark

when the light
sends my shadow away
I'll keep the sensation
that for a tiny moment
I held to something
of me

and in the end
if I cannot understand
my shadow
at least I will know
that we danced

a day with the dog

me and the dog
are reading the morning paper

actually she's flat out
asleep
by my feet on the veranda

me and the dog
are settling accounts on the computer

actually she's flat out
asleep
blocking the corridor

but really
she goes like the clappers
if there's breakfast
in the wind
and she woofs a throaty call
sometimes
to the sky
she saves her energy and her run
for when she knows she'll get good mileage
like for a nature call
or
anytime there's food

me and the dog
are watching football on the TV

actually she's flat out
asleep
lying down in the lounge room

me and the dog
we're up late reading

actually she's flat out
a-snooze
on my bedroom floor

it's time for this poem
to sleep

2015 (2)

who is the girl?

I am the girl
who spread her wings
in the treetops

I am the girl
who has tamed the wind
for flight

it was me you saw
I
blocked the stars out

I am the girl
who's just like a bird
and I fly

~

I am the girl
swims like a fish
in the river

I am the girl
who pushes water
aside

it was me who danced
beneath the flash
of the sunlight

I am the girl
the stream and the river
are mine

~

the wind
cannot blow me
away from my path

the river
washes over
then
it is past

I am the one
that the flames
can't consume

I'm the girl
the day is mine
it's my turn

~

I am the girl
who walked naked
into fire

I am the girl
poked her tongue
at the coals

it was me behind
the fiddle the day
that rome baked

I am the girl
and I have no match
but
I burn

wild

wild thing in the sky

> *blow my hat around*
> *send me stumbling*
> *like an old man*
> *in a hot pursuit*

wild thing in the sky

> *fill my raincoat up*
> *flapping like a ghost*
> *trying to frighten me*
> *in daytime*

wild thing in the sky

> *blow my thoughts away*
> *raise them in the air*
> *like a paper bag*
> *like a bird*

wild thing in the sky

> *come toy with me*
> *play me like a four string*
> *and sing a-woo*
> *old man stumbling*

huntsman (three strikes)

when I opened my eyes
he was there
trying for inconspicuous
on the ceiling

I said

> *hello*
> *I see you*
> *don't be there when I come home*
> *don't make yourself*
> *a target*

when I sat in my easy chair
I saw him
faux blending with the curtains
by the wall

I said

> *hello*
> *I see you*
> *I'll let it slide but*
> *you better not show*
> *when I'm here again*

when I reached for the kettle
I nearly jumped
he was guarding the switch
and the power

I said

> *hello*
> *your time has come*

I put him in a jam jar
and flew him down to the garden

I said

> *goodbye*
> *I guess I'll see you around*
> *just remember three strikes*
> *and then you're gone*

moon and light

big yellow moon
heavy in the sky
stars don't shine
as brightly

old yellow moon
smaller every day
more stars bright
in darkness

small yellow moon
sickle in the night
stars shine swirls
and spatters

no yellow moon
darkness to my eye
stars shine white
where are you

hey lunar light
silver to my skin
starlight shines
inside me

wind song

    w-ooo woo-woo-woo

the whistling of the wind

    wooo woo-woo-woo

listen to her sing

twirling leaves up in the trees
laughing while she ruffles me

    h-ooo woo-woo-woo

little kisses on my skin

    hoo woo-woo

wish that I was on the wing

watch me flying cross the sky
climb and soar and sway and glide

    hoo-woo-woo-woo

the calling of the wind

    hoo-woo-woo-woo

listen to her sing

    hoo   *hoo-woo-woo*

the doggy in the morning

light a fire for the doggy
so she can sleep all nice and warm
she's been woof-ing at three-thirty
instead of snoozing all night long

woof woof woof

I have to get up for the doggy
to take her out into the cold
she'll woof me up about three-thirty
chill me to my bones

woof woof woof

the doggy thinks that it is playtime
the doggy's having fun
she's woofing me up about three-thirty
when sleep is all I want

woof woof woof

going to trick that doggy
she won't know what's going on
I'll woof her up about three-thirty
before she's got her sleeping done

woof woof woof

hungry dog

give me some breakfast
give me three
I'm as hungry
as can be
I will eat
till there's no more
give me some breakfast
give me four

should I wake you
in the night
because this hunger
is not right
it makes me moan
and makes me howl
think I'll wake you up
right now

second best
I'll lick a plate
hurry your eating
don't make me wait
please be sure
to leave some crumbs
second best
just leave me one

give me some supper
now's the time
I will bark
until it's mine
can't spend all day
just lying round
give some supper
to your hound

or I will wake you
up midnight
mine the hunger
yours the plight
if I can't eat
then you can't snore
wake you up
to give me more

woof you up
to get some more

goodnight moonlight

I stood on the moon
and turned out the lights
one

by

one

a pinch of my fingers
and darkness comes
soon

there's

none

the stars that twinkled
have gone to sleep
a hug and a kiss their dreams to keep

the flickering sky
is safe in bed
hush hush and goodnight my sleepy head

I stood on the moon
and turned out the lights
one

by

one

and soon

there's

none

amaze me

sweep me up into your arms
when I am paying no attention

pen a poem in my name
on the napkin in a restaurant

climb onto a table
sing a song that urges revolution

then dance me
on a pavement of promises
across the road
to make traffic stop

spin me around like an idea
you've just formed
make me feel that I'm right there
in a dream
with you

read me a chapter from the book
of your life that you are writing

show me the half-painted canvas
that holds an image of my face

hold me close against your skin
so I am one with your rhythm beating

then raise me
in the air on a whispered word
that I can fly
like a thought released

2015 (2)

fluttered round like a desire
you've just encountered
make me feel that I'm right there
in the dream
with you

rain catching

to catch all of the rain
in a bowl made of glass
just chase each droplet around

or hold out your tongue
to catch one on the end
and chase each droplet around

oh they say that the wind
will blow storms cross the sky
so chase each droplet around

watch all the weather
from cloud down to heather
and chase every droplet around

the solo dancer attempts an explanation

my brethren
I see you are moved by the wind
and even I must sway

but do you hear
the sound that fills up my heart

the wind is such a shallow thing
it moves us once
and then it goes

but are we not deep-tuned
to a different song

do you not sense
in the earth
the vibration
of a restless need somewhere

are you not touched by the caress
of the soil that holds us

I can feel the tremble of love

I can feel low fire

I hear music in the core
inside me
and I have to dance

brethren
watch me move

brothers-sisters feel the chord
delve a little deeper
find the vibration
we all are seeking

brothers-sisters
know the heartbeat
even if just the once
then
let yourself go

sweet and slow

when I stop
listening to my own heartbeat

when I stop
hearing the noises in the air

when I stop
the constant chirp inside my eardrums

I can place my hand on the ground
to listen through my fingertips
the sweet slow *feeling* of sound

I can listen
from *underneath* the water

I can listen
with my head raised in the air

I can listen
a man caught up in feedback

or just place my hand on the ground
and draw it up
through my fingers

the sweet slow feeling
of sound

golden slumber

unquietly he slumbers

> *sometimes a twitch*
>
> *sometimes a grumble*
>
> *sometimes he moves an arm*
> *or a shoulder*
>
> *writhes*
> *'til he rests no more*

lava beneath him
golden pillow for his head

sleep
you earth
you magma

stay the fire
in your dreams

sleep

hush

hush a little

> *there is a moth*
> *banging on the window*

hush a little

> *is that rain*
> *tumbling on the rooftop*

and hush a little

> *can you hear*
> *a cup of tea is calling*

hush

the night is quiet
it is peaceful in my bed

have you listened

I saw a woman in the forest
drape herself around a tree
she turned to see me watching
said

have you listened to them breathe

she said

*these trees will take up water
precious life through every vein
if you come up close and still your heartbeat
it's like a shushing in your dreams*

*from the roots up to the branches
water flows then turns into air
and if you hold them close enough for hearing
the pulse of trees of life is kin to prayer*

to breathe

he pours a little drink
raises his glass
casts an eye at the spare
on the table

he never can be sure
on these cold black nights
will she come back
this time

so there's wine in her glass
while he lifts up his own
in a silent toast
and drinks deep
against the evil chance

and when she does get home
a little later
just as he knew she would
he says he poured it for her
early
to let it breathe

then tips himself another
to sip with her
warm before the fire

the cold night can wait —
bitter —
outside again

six ways to measure time (on a visit to the big smoke)

being overtaken on a six-lane
by a truck in a hurry
to gain a single car length
before turning off the freeway
at the next off-ramp

> *noticing the courtesy of a reporter*
> *who has taken to the skies in a helicopter*
> *to inform drivers caught in traffic*
> *they are in a jam*

we two holding hands in a run
flat out
across one half of the pedestrian crossing
to then stall at the lights
in the centre of the road

> *jaw-dropping at the billboards*
> *advertising a new allotment of residential land*
> *going cheap*
> *where the revered green-belt*
> *used to be*

recalling one of the places
that I used to live in
while circling and unsure
in the new-built roundabout

2015 (2)

getting a third song –
an old favourite –
in the encore
when I had only expected
one

song of a road

judder
judder
judder
judder jive
(the corrugations)

the thin white stripes
are an undulating song
that slip apart
as they sing nearer
then bleed into the flying wing
that is the leading edge
of the car
as we gaze a-stare
with mesmer-eyes fixed upon
the next approaching verse

the miles a chant
each town the same
a chorus of the small

quickly look . . .

but did you see . . .

well no . . .

it is gone . . .

there'll be another
in a little while

the 'S' that is a solid line
becomes a bridge
becomes a river

becomes the *'Slow Down'*
of a railway level crossing
going nowhere in both directions

there is no train
just a
used to be
beside the highway

and the bitumen is again
a semibreve of rests
and intervening spaces
in the song
that is the road

we are eating up
these miles

first salt

the first sight of salt water
an inlet
is almost justification enough
for the tedious uprooting
and interminable travel
on this journey from the inland
to a city
via the sea

six hours through mountains
snow and sleet behind
incessant soaking drizzle
and squalls that howl like banshee ghosts
with their accompanying gusts
a constant buffet and a beating

but here at the town of *Robe*
by the seaside
with much of the journey done
the wind is
of the sea
and the rippling waves
shivering the inlet
are patterns
immediately familiar
and the bringers
of a sense of peace
not known back in the hills of home

the first sight of salt water
changes the nature of the wind
until it blows
not winter fury
but stories
from distant shores
to be inhaled

absorbed

tomorrow will be
a new city

at Koko Black

1)

    that's magnificent

here we are in Koko Black
the noir is in this chocolate
the noir is in these beans
the noir is in the lighting
barely more than
Koko Black

    that's my kind of coffee

in Koko Black
the dark is in no-need-to-ask
the dark is in brown swirls
the dark is in the colour
of the waiter's threads so
Koko Black

2)

    rake thin

he looks like the model last month
on the cover of Vogue
slim jeans
long legs
a flounce
that is a shawl across his shoulder
beneath the pony tail

he stalks this salon

    klick-klack

in high boots
of patent leather
he stalks the floors

hard-dainty
like a proprietor
of the air
in Koko Black

3)

this is a jewel shop

each piece
has a special place

    walnut cluster
    cinnamon
    raspberry
    Bailey's

centres are displayed
laid out on velvet

dark brown on black

    oh yes
    which one did you try
    oh yes
    this piece is special oh
    oh yes-s-s

this one for you
is a piece
of Koko Black

the escaping

the escapologist
has concluded his act

carefully
carefully
he un-kinks each link
in a yellow length of chain
coils it into a convenient backpack
for his tools

undoes every buckle
of the canvas straight-jacket
folds it small
then tucks it
into a purple bowler hat
and into the backpack
before he leaves
to trade a place
for a place
a little further up the Mall
from which he will escape
again

washing a day

there's a puddle from the rain
filling like a lake
on the footpath

a ripple through the middle
might have been a fish
could have been
a fly

but it's really just the weather
falling from the sky again
pointillism on a window glass

watching the washing
of a day

another week or so
it will be clean

2015 (3)

old traffic stoppers

I can see men who were young
in *my* old man's day

overalls supporting bellies
and holding forth
with their opinionated views

in the middle of the street

yesterday
stopping traffic
as today tries
to find a way
around them

two Kookaburras

two Kookaburras
share a branch
this once
but they hunt
with back facing back

a perch
perhaps
a perch maybe

but the killing ground
is each
on its own

modestly (begun)

I modestly approach the light of day
stand naked against the window
the frost spreads out an ice-capade
the clouds wear grey frowns
and the sun is gradually lightening
for the morning just begun

a neighbouring rooster starts the clock
each tick towards a brighter hour
one more call is to awaken me
another crow for stretching out
with the third and last the frost is a-glow
and a light that draws me on

through the glass
I'm dancing across ice
leave footprints behind me
in the grass

laughing with the kookaburra —
cackling like a fool —
I twirl around and round
beneath the clouds

who can say this day
has not begun

so
modestly I throw wide my arms
cavort naked beneath the elder tree
a bower bird imitates her song
and a grey thrush trills a tune
my kookaburra sings her song and laughs
and I
have just begun

flashing

my fish will swim through oceans
they will flash their shiny tails
when they turn

when they turn

they will flash their shiny tails
when they turn

my birds will fly in blue skies
they will flash their coloured feathers
on the wing

on the wing

they will flash their coloured feathers
on the wing

my fish will swim through blue skies
they will flash their shiny feathers
on the wing

when they fly

they flash their shiny feathers
on the wing

my birds will fly in oceans
they will flash their coloured tails
when they turn

on the wing

they will flash their coloured tails
when they turn

remove my hat

from the grey
the turmoil
here they fall
in their thousands

is the flight
exhilaration
do they glide

or does the wind
confuse them
to collide in hundreds
as they fall

through a ray
of stray light
in their tens
their decads

a mission full of purpose
or a slip
a trip
a stumble
how did it all begin
well
who can say

the lone fallen droplet
at my feet
pursues it's brother/sisters
I remove my hat
from on my head
for those that fell

the poem insomnia

I am
in conversation with myself
talking to
an imaginary you

I call my thought
a stanza
my big idea
a poem
and every word you say to me
is said in rhyme
yes
all the time

I'm imaginary versing
with my unreal you
responding to some thing
you didn't say

I call your thought
a couplet
your small idea
haiku

well bless you
I said in rhyme
and bless you
all the time

it's fun to talk to you
inside my head
in big ideas
announced at an open-mic
when I can't sleep

I named my poem
insomnia
and it was good to read you there
to make me rhyme
all the time

porch or veranda

this is
the first time I have sat here
without the dog

she was old when we first arrived
since then
we've chewed some bones
brewed our coffee
drunk some wine

she passed away last Autumn
I've ventured out in Spring
it won't be long
and I'll be gone
to sit beneath some other porch
some other veranda

I'll leave the dog
in her happy home
beneath a sway of leaves
and I
I will keep moving on

the tree is to bird is to tree is to

the busy-ness of birds
defines the purpose
of the tree

for why is a branch
if not a perch

for what the leaves
if not
to conceal

the being of the tree
defines the modus
of the bird

for where to spy the worm
if not from height
if not from perpendicular
to the ground

and for why
the reflexive clasp
if not for branches

Spring sound

I can almost hear the sap rise
to push the flowers on the fruit trees
open

or maybe it's the sound of bees
buzzing impatiently
while they wait for bounty

a cockatoo is *crack*-ing
and a honey-eater squeaks
even the house is stretching out
behind me

lazy clouds luff quiet by
below the sun
above me
here where I make these scratches
with my pen
almost as loud
as Springtime

Wangaratta tandem

a big woman in her forties
embedded into a mobility scooter
rips through pedestrian traffic
then pulls smartly to the side of the footpath
in a well-practiced manoeuvre

gives a deep
wet
smokers cough
filled with old history and current intent

her partner
a pinch-faced weed in his fifties
pulls in behind her
dismounts his steed

too much emphysema to walk
he staggers to the steps
of the *lottery* and *sundry goods* shop

comes out a few moments later
with a quick-pick
and a packet of forty

they both light up

    ahh

    ahh

power up and they're off
in tandem
down the centre of the pavement

2015 (3)

cigarette
in hand and mouth
feeling lucky

    let's go
    grab a pizza

be-bop night

I'm kept awake
by the sound of frogs

here I am —
up late —
when I should be sleeping

the gnats and the mites that fly
around the room
circle my lampshade
crash into my window
from the outside

disconcert my peace
with their desire for the warm
that is my light

but when I embrace the dark
to guide me towards sleeping
I hear the frogs
be-bop
earnest in their crying need

> *the water's here*
> *be bop*
> *the reeds are near*
> *be-bop*
> *the Summer is so early*

2015 (3)

come to me my froggy queen
come to me my dear
be-bop
be-bop
this night is made for love

at least
that is how I hear them

I'm kept awake
the bugs are fried
but the frogs play
at merry gentlemen

to defy

the sun is white
the sun is yellow
the sun is red

> *I close my eyes*
> *the sun stares into me*

a-glow around the solar orb
the sun is belching
life

> *I better stay inside the house*
> *or I might die*

a fizz around the diminished star
and the sun is bubbling
death

> *each ray to kiss my skin*
> *keeps me alive*

and I stare into the eye
the sun
defied

still - rising

it's a slow slow day
I'm watching rain

there are two still snails
on the wall

I'm reading in time
with the steady fall

three still snails
are on the go

slow day siren call
rain spatter my page

four snails still
and yet rising

to love you is . . .

what I was meant for, and
all that I've wanted
the bright in a sun-shining day

and you are . . .
my reason for rising
the meaning when I sing
the feeling that moves me to say

that I love to . . .
hold you so close, and
help you feel warm
keep our cold moments away

and what I was meant for
is you
and what I have wanted is too
you're my reason to rise
and I sing so your eyes shine
I want to hold you so close you'll feel warm
no matter the cold
or the storm

stab and howl

the night is stabbed
by a distant light
and though I do not hear
the thunder
I know the sound of that bilious growl
that can fill the dark
with wonder

stabbed once more
but the night won't die in gouts of pain
it is roaring
between the bellow and the night
the storm prevails
on and on it howls
until morning

flash mob in Deniliquin

we are the *sunshine-wimoweh*
ukulele flash mob

sunshine wimoweh
we are ukulele mob

flash mob sunshine
ukulele and wimoweh

creeping through the village
to you

sun-flash
shine mob
here we come with *wimoweh*

wim-mob
oweh-flash
our sunshine will bright the day

sunshine and flash mob
ukulele's here to stay

wimoweh-wimoweh
a-wimoweh-a-wimoweh wimoweh-a-wimoweh

hush, there's a bear . . .

will you please stay here quietly
my bear, my bear

OF COURSE I WILL
JUST LET ME BANG THE DOOR CLOSED
I WON'T MAKE A SINGLE SOUND
YOUR QUIET BEAR
I AM

will you be ursa hush-a-bye
dear bear, my dear bear

WHY, CERTAINLY
I HAVE ONLY THESE FEW
POTS AND PANS
TO GENTLE INTO THEIR PLACE
AND YOU WON'T KNOW YOUR BEAR
IS EVEN NEAR

will you be teddy bear, the silent one
oh bear, my dear bear

YES INDEED
I'LL GUARD YOUR DOOR
FROM ANY NOISE
I WILL GROWL AND GROWL FOR QUIET
SHOULD ANYONE INTRUDE
I WILL BE YOUR GUARDING BEAR

AND WOULD YOU LIKE ME
TO SOOTHE AND SNUFFLE YOU
TO SLEEP
WATCH OVER YOU AND COMFORT YOU

YOUR BEAR
YOUR VERY
QUIET
bear

meeting Nola

oh god

she said

oh christ

the three steps
loomed
looked set to defeat her

bony fragility
her walking aid an impediment
to balance
she leaned against the rail
and grasped
with both hands
and a tremble

oh lord

he noticed the desperation
the death-grip on the railing
the bunching of stocking around each ankle

can I help

a slow pivot
to release one hand
for a lunging clutch
onto his arm

the music starts
at one o'clock
oh christ

the a low peregrination
up three steps
arm-in-arm
and along the uneven path
trembling grasp translated
into the vice-like grip
of the frail afraid

in the auditorium doorway
a long look of assessment
at avenues through seating
and the location of friends
before glancing up

my name
is Nola

who are you

in Daylesford, the news

and hey-hey well
the news comes slow
to Daylesford
even though *The Age* newspaper is here
on time

the lead story
about the caliphate
and the one about the power-line fire
have to fight for time
on the footpath
where the eggs and bacon are in possession
of the street
and it's the cutlery that sounds
all the updates

and hey
the French are searching Hungary
for a bomber
maybe the bombs are hidden away
beneath the coffee cups
within the baby-cino froth
in-between the shouted words
of Saturday bonhomie
or walking through the traffic
of a Daylesford street
to buy the raffle for the CFA

hey-hey-hey
surely the sport pages would do better
except for little dogs
in groups of three
and big boys on the pavement

Ambrosia —
the pug —
reads from his mama's lap
but only snorts

the Big Bash Cricket League
is not the main game
never the main game
in Daylesford

harlequin blue-tongue

shy blue-tongue
curl away
and curl away
shine your scales
like harlequin diamonds
in the sun

2016 (1)

into sleep

fade me to sleep
take
my breath away
lead me to dream
catch
my heart in your sway

and sing me goodnight
wish up
on a star

take me to darkness
to sleep
where you are

hot

A-1 hellish sun
string your rays for strum-pets
play in tune
from night until noon
burn us up like
flambé-ettes

a silky leap of starlings

ten starlings in the silky oak
can't rest
amid a boon of nectar

bounce

they bounce
from flower to flower
to chatter
and screech
and hector
and
lift off
into a balletic plane
they soar
the nectar pumping

around
around
they wheel and wheel
then back
to the orange silky oak

where they —
those shining
vulgaris starlings —
why
each of them
is jumping

shaman

he has died

he has been born

he is a trance
that can turn into
a swallow
that will fly
with every beat
pounded on the drum

he is the word on the page
that turns to magic
these small
fleet
thoughts

but he had to die
so this
could be made

in the path of a fire

House 1

Vacant.

House 2

M1, I don't want to alarm you
but there is a bushfire close by.

If I tell you to move, you must move quickly.

M1.: Oh, well,
thank you Frank, that's very kind,
but I don't care about fire.

God doesn't care
about fire, and I have to listen
to God.

House 3

B., and **D.**, I don't want to alarm you
but there is a bushfire close by.

If I tell you to move, you must move quickly.

D.: Yes Nurse.

B.: Right-o, Franky.

House 4

M2., C., and S.,
I don't want to alarm you
but there is a bushfire close by.

If I tell you to move, you must move quickly.

M2: (sings) . . . burn for you
what else am I going to do . . .

S.: They've lit the fire
to make me get out
of here.

No-one wants me here.
They hate me.

Why do they all
hate me?

C.: Oh, Mister Frank,
you frightened me.
I didn't know you were standing there.
a-ha-ha-ha-ha.

you frightened me.

C. proceeds, half-dressed,
to the smoking shed
and lights up a gasper.

She wears slacks
and sports a flagging bath towel
under her arms
to support decorum
and modesty.

House 5

Vacant.

House 6

P., **B.**, and **M3.**, I don't want to alarm you
but there is a bushfire close by.

If I tell you to move, you must move quickly.

P.: Can I have a cigarette?

B.: I love you Frank. You
look after me.

I love all the nurses here. They all
look after me.

M3.: (trembling violently in his chair) Can I have
a Seroquel? My nerves . . .
they're playing up.

They're just no good.

House 7

T., and **N.**, I don't want to alarm you
but there is a bushfire close by.

If I tell you to move, you must move quickly.

T.: That doesn't matter Nurse Heinz. Paul
is coming at one o'clock
and he is going to take me to Albury
and we'll have a big house there
and three children.

N.: (nods her head) Yes nurse.
She looks deep into my eyes, and smiles
with the innocence
of a child.

autumn leaving

a leaf took a dive
from the top of the oak
and it flew

then it fell

branch to branch

it flitted and it fluttered
in cavort
as it came down

kissing every twig

goodbye

goodbye

descended into clear space
took it's aim
and used the air
to steer a path
by luff
on luff

until it landed
not on earth
as I'd thought it had in mind
no
it rested right upon
my face

eejit magpie

eejit!
tromping over new sod

eejit
I've turned the sprinkler on!

ya eejit!
why're you fluffing your black feathers

eejit
is that a clean-your-feathers song

eejit
splashing in the puddles

you're an *eejit*
seems like you're having too much fun

for an *eejit*
you've done alright on a hot day

who is the *eejit*
when you've ended
with a worm

barefoot

I go barefoot
on bedroom carpet
drag my heels
push each strand down

phlitt phlitt

morning shuffle

I go barefoot
on kitchen vinyl
cool and smooth
the indoor pond

sheee sheee

breakfast shuffle

I go barefoot
on waving green grass
bended blades
a meadow walk

shush shush

lush lawn shuffle

I go barefoot
on garden woodchips
softest sponge
contoured steps

2016 (1)

kraa kraa

vegie shuffle

phlitt
sheee
shush
kraa

that's the way I shuffle

space debris

I will sweep between the stars
and littered spaces
with a broom
the bristling broom
upon my broom
I will clean away the debris
in those interstellar niches

and when the deep
is dark and wide and clear again
I will turn my face
to home

I will sweep around the sun
and the cratered moon
with the broom
the *vroomy vroom*
that is my broom
I will clean away the debris
of my circum-solar journey

and when the sky
is gold and milk and clear again
I will turn my face
towards home

2016 (1)

I will sweep across the land
and the ocean blue
upon that broom
high flying broom
my sky-high broom
I will clean away the debris
from all interstitial spaces

and when the land
and ocean deep are clean again
I will turn my face
towards home

step inside fourteen

she is fair
she is loud
she is sixty

the bottle blond
shuffles from her bedroom
to the kitchen
singing a facsimile
of Cilla Black

> *step inside love*
> *come my way*
> *ooh*
> *step inside love*
> *come and stay*

she interrupts herself
to drag my attention away
from dishing out lunchtime meds

> *Fra-ank*
> *my father is coming for my birthday*
>
> *is my father coming for my birthday?*
>
> *it's my sixteenth birthday*
> *no*
> *my fourteenth birthday*

she laughs

2016 (1)

I've been fourteen for a long time

I'm always fourteen

I'll be fourteen when I die

Fra-ank
do you think people live forever
do they come back after they die

I think they do

is my father going to come
for my birthday?

step inside love
step inside love
come my way

stitch winter

I like to do
my stitching to the light of the sun
the cold cold light of the sun
coming through my window

it's all chilly-bones outside
and the rain seems laced with ice
the days have crept July
but I am warm here while I stitch
a little picture
of winter

unless . . .

your husband just dragged rubbish in
while you were making tidy
and everywhere his footsteps went
he's dragged the mud behind him

but
then he roasted coffee beans
just like you hoped he would
rich and dark brown coffee beans
that look and smell so good

he's living in a world apart
when you really need him here
he's hiding in the garden shed
when you want him he's nowhere

until he grinds the coffee beans
just like you thought he should
rich and dark brown coffee beans
that make you feel so good

he's neglected shopping once again
he's failed to tend to the chores
no he hasn't thought of anything
can you take this anymore

unless
he's cooked those coffee beans
the way you knew he could
rich and dark brown coffee beans
that make you
feel
so good

calling out salt

I call my cow from kilometres away
she runs when I call out salt

    S-A~A-A-L-T

my cow bellows out from kilometres away
she bellows when she hears me calling salt

    S-A~A-A-L-T
    S-A~A-A-L-T

I know where my cow is though kilometres away
she's waiting for my call of salt

    S-A~A-A-L-T

she runs right home
for salt

    S-A~A-A-L-T

    S-A~A-A-L-T

Mister Frank – simply the best

mister frank is the very best nurse
mister frank is a great nurse
la la la la
mister frank

she calls me Mister Frank
and I call her Miss Shirley

I'm not sure why Mister Frank
is rating so well today
but
I think I can handle it all right

maybe it's because I dish out
the pills
more likely
because I remind her
what she's ordered for lunch
and sympathise
about how many showers she's had to take today
how often she's had to change her bedding
wash the clothes
the sweeping
the relentless demands
on her time and her mental stamina
working working
working
all in the space of a single day . . .

at least
that's her story

it can be tiring just to listen
to the litany of burden
but today I've made the effort

and as a result I can see
that Mister Frank is clearly
the best

> *Mister Frank*
> *can I have a cigarette*

keyed all alone

she said

> I used to keep a spare key out
> underneath the loose brick
> but then I threw that man I had
> out into the night
>
> and I started thinking
> what if
> one day
> what if someone found it
> would they break inside
> and threaten me
>
> I'm a woman alone
>
> but the reason I moved the key
> I suppose
> was the thought that maybe
> he'd come back
> and help himself
> to what's not his anymore
>
> the other day I went to work
> my two door-keys in the kitchen
> on the table
>
> locked out

Frank Prem

when I came home that night
I smoked a cigarette in blue smoke
sat on the chair that I placed
on the porch
and I wondered

about being a woman
alone

elementals

I will rain across Red Cliff
there's no dry within my song
no dry
in my song
I will rain down

        I will burn over Stanhope
        the Sun is never wrong
        the Sun
        does no wrong
        I will burn

I will fall down on Mildura
no drought will still my song
no drought
still my song
I will fall down

        I'll bake brown Dimboola
        Where clouds do not belong
        the clouds
        do not belong
        I will bake them

I will slake thirst in Echuca
        I will dust down Strathmerton
sweet river sing the song
        and blow the dirt along

river
        red dirt
sing the song
        roll along

I will   *I*

slake   ***will***

you***blow***

the old lady's parrot

I should ring the old lady

> there's a parrot
> in your chimney

ring the old lady

> there's a parrot

on the phone

why's an old lady
got a parrot
in her chimney
if I don't ring the old lady
well I guess I'll never know

> Mrs. old lady
> you've got a parrot
> in your chimney

> Mrs. old lady
> I had to call you
> on the phone

> Mrs. old lady
> why's a parrot
> in your chimney
> oh
> I'm sorry Mrs. Lady
> I guess you didn't know

a parrot in the chimney
a parrot on the phone
a parrot's not a symphony
and I thought
you ought
to know

2016 (2)

the terrible malady of Miss Shirl

Mister Frank
oh Mister Frank
I've been so crook

I was sick and sick and sick
and sick

I was soooo
sick Mister Frank

I died last night
I was completely dead
yes yes
but I came alive again

three days later

ha ha ha
ha

how are you
Mister Frank
are you all right?

gravity

I fell

like a drop of rain
like a snowflake
like a yellow autumn leaf
like a stone
or a waterfall
an avalanche

I fell like there was no choice

I fell from here
into the heart of the world

a sketch of the season

here come clouds
they're running grey
on white
under blue

trees are a silhouette
black
in a three-D foreground
still as night
in the heart of a picture
of mid-winter

a semblance that remains

charcoal on cartridge paper

ink applied with a twig

wash blackened-water
with the grungiest brush

a blob puts some form
on a curved line

black placed just there
was meant as grey

never mind never mind
the model is fixed now
upon your paper
and at the end
when time's over
the man walks away from you
but
his image
remains

self portrait via life-draw

I have charcoaled a man

I am inking a woman

he wears a short goatee
and no distinctive features

she bears a tattoo
that adorns the skin of her back
like remnant lace
from the rumple of a negligee
tossed carelessly away

his head is drawn as round as a circle
and overly tiny

I find proportion
is not a sense that I possess
at all

her hair has proved impossible to tame
and over-flows a poor arrangement
barely held in place
by a green rubber band

these pictures —
my scribbles scrawls and scratches —
are impressed on the now-smudged white
of a sheet of cartridge paper
but . . .

always somehow
it seems I rend them better
penned and then re-worked
into the phrases I find most familiar
until
here I am
etching a silhouette of myself again
charcoaled and inked
into queer shaped stanzas

this drawing from life
is not really a new thing
it seems it's just another portrait
in the usual words
that are me

that *I* am

truck canyon alarm clock (good morning)

the trucks that roll down Mellish Street
take lumber from the hills above the town
that are plantations

and their rumble and their roar project
in an illusion that seems to run for miles
through the Spring Creek canyon

in a funny way
an inexplicable way
the engines bellow is soothing
in the heart of night-time
in the early morning

it echoes like the sound of a faded dream
that stops
just before the call . . .

> *good morning you*
> *see the sun rise*
> *wake up and shine*
> *shine*
> *shine*

. . . of the quarter to six
alarm clock

fetching the firewood

all through the sogginess of winter
with the water high
above my heels
I carted the rounds of sliced timber

knotted rotten or smooth
I moved them
load upon load

once
into the barrow
once
into the cart
once more
into the barrow
then last
into a pile
a bloody great big pile
of a former tree
that I could hardly stand
to look at
anymore

filled
with witchety grubs
overflowing
white ants
a-crawl
with slater bugs
and centipedes

some geckos

2016 (2)

and now
the weather smiling
and the ground firm
under my feet again

I take my splitting tool in hand
to separate each round
into component firewood

each round
into a sweet sigh
when it is cold outside

yes it's true
what my father told me
those years ago

> *that wood*
> *my son*
> *that wood is going to warm you*
> *five times*
> *before it's gone*

but by my count
it's six

laughing

the big man laughed
with a big man's laugh

    HA HA HAHA HA
    HA HA HAHA HA

his belly trembled
and the earth
re-bound
jiggled and jangled
to that resonant sound

    HA HAHA HA
    HA HAHA HA

a little old lady
had a little old laugh

    tee hee teehee hee
    tee hee teehee hee

her shoulders shook
and the clock unwound
chimes started tingling
all around this town

    tee hee teehee hee
    tee hee teehee hee

ukulele nights

ukulele nights
ukulele days
sing gentle in the quiet
sing gentle in this place

play inside a sigh
touch the string that way
ukulele nights
ukulele days

in six small stanzas

(1)

That was a good reading.
I like your work.
Could we get a drink,
by ourselves somewhere,
discuss mine?

(2)

This house is wonderful,
so many places to choose.
Serve me first
on the island bench
in the kitchen.
Eat me.

(3)

I know it's midnight, but,
do you always
come to your door naked?
Shut up.
I want to make you come at your door,
naked.

(4)

. . .
. . .
. . .
mmm.

(5)

Do you ever write
about the white-caps
slow-moving
all across the Bay?

(6)

This
is
the   last
time.

I am
done

with
fucking

poetry.

Listening to Gariwerd

god of the mountain

who was it
that walked these hills
and with a stamp of his feet
shuddered the stone
to shingle

who lit the blaze
beneath the land
to turn this mountain
into a cone filled with fire

I see the signs
but I do not know

the blue-grey haze
obscures me

yet when the sun
on the sandstone in the evening
glows red
I can almost see a face —
like the picture of a man —
in the mountain

Frank Prem

sniffing the cusp of Spring

sniffing the cusp of Spring . . .

and the smell I smell
is the green of grass

the blue of the hills

and the sundry orange
of gazanias
on roadside verges

meadow daisy white
and the yellow lush
that is new clover

marsupials, maternals, matriarchs

the kangaroo is in the paddock

> *the kangaroos are in the paddock*

the joey has left his mama

> *the joeys have left their mamas*

one is hopping on the green grass

> *they all are hopping on the green grass*

the marsupials rule

> *marsupials*
> *rule*

gnarly country

I am not *observing* it
I am *in* it

and it looms
peering down on me

assessing
while the water falls
single drops and rivulets
of white noise
and judgement

Listening to Gariwerd

an unseen presence - I waiting - the wren

the grey wren
is under supervision
from a superb blue

they have alighted
four times this morning
on the balcony
and the grey
has flown to the top
of a glass door
only to slide

    tap

    tap

    tap

    tap

    flutter

to the ground

again
and again

then away for a few moments
before return to try again

the blue
is supportively close at hand
seeming to urge the grey
to greater effort
to success
to *triumph*

then away

they seem to feel the influence
of an unseen presence

something handsome . . .

attractive

as near
as the other side of the glass
where I stand

watching
and waiting

free-verse song

I wonder
does a schizophren-iac
have music in his head
like I do

does he use his medication
to dull the bass

>   DOOF DOOF
>   *DOof DOof*
>   *Doof*
>   *doof*

for I cannot think
unaccompanied
and I cannot write
alone

a tune sails by
across the wave-wash
that is my mind
then
I am singing free-verse
onto paper

lunching at The Kookaburra Hotel

he's a big boy

a tousled
honey blonde
ranga

drinks a big beer-jar

let's call it
a schooner

he is eating pancakes
with his girl
and has emptied the maple syrup

looking around for honey

she is still picking at her mains
while he
is already dessert down

> *maple syrup*
> *honey crepe*
> *and you my dear*

lunch is going down well
today

that hare o' mine

my hare has very large ears
she leaps
I call her *bounder*

she goes to sleep
in a grassy hide
and listens to the world
around her

my hare has very large ears
she runs
the wind behind her

she zigs and she zags
all across the field
but won't come when I call
confound her

my hare has very large ears
she twitches
and her nose is wrinkles

she can smell when I
am waiting nearby
but she is coy and I don't
understand her

my hare
with the very large ears

framed sketch at the Harvest café/restaurant

at Fyan's Creek

flotsam
is a catastrophe
of tree trunks and branches

water sculpture
is built that way

the still pond trembles —
a-shiver —
in rippled moments
every time the breeze stops by
to whisper of romance

and the flies buzz of droning sleep
bidding you *rest awhile*
the frog calls *bomp*
bomp
as you teeter into a dream
of creek contentment

did a fish jump
an eel twist . . .

did the yabby wave
with a claw

>   *goodbye*
>   *call again*

with a waving claw

>   *goodbye*
>   *please call again*

small, like yesterday

yesterday I climbed
The Pinnacle
the land was so small
below

cockatoos
minute points of white
wheeling

slow gliding
above the blue blur
that was the forest

today
now
I am in the basin land
as low down
as I can be

towering above
scarcely visible
amid the crags
of rough mountain
a tiny sandstone finger
points out

and I think that I can see
my effigy
moving on a platform
that is as small
as yesterday

observations

lunch
under a brooding mountain

lichen
inhabiting a tree

wild fruit
on the brink of bloom

the waitress is on special
and . . .

there is *you*

the eucalypt is colour-tinged
on its leaf tips

the corella cries loudly
as it flies

a feather of cloud hangs
in a sea of blue

the silence here
is a thing alivet

allowed

one hundred faces etched
in stone
the *Maui* of these mountains
gaze at me

the wind and rain
have shaped for years
to carve such a jury

to judge *me*
stepping —
jump to jump —
between rock ledges

me
trying to get some breath
into my lungs
as air

me
unworthy man
trying to scale the heights
to be above them

they judge me
and weigh my path

are they benign?
they do not say so

are they unquiet?
the wind agrees

are they really there?
there is something

are they in my mind?
they speak

and I can hear them
as clear as clapping thunder

I must go on
until I peak
upon *The Pinnacle*

I am here
they have allowed me

unworthy man
and yet
allowed

A Blue-Tongued Lizard Life

conquering heroes

ack ark   ark ack

ark ack   ack ark

for months we have been
alternately entertained
and irritated
by the endless rearing
of magpie chicks

squaw   squaw
*   squaw-squaw   squuaw squaw*

squawking for parental attention

petulant and sulky
lost and disarranged
demanding and self-entitled

the younger generation
have kept their elders
on their talons
and at their tasks

now
in high summer
they are adult —
barely adult —
stalking their home ground
in a gang of six or more

ack ark   *ark ack*

ark ack   *ack ark*

four in a square
they are organized

serially croaking

gradually progressing
to the far end of their territory

each in turn
stepping toward the centre
to croak and hurriedly offer a peck
before retreat to the periphery

at the heart
of their formation
is the subject
of their unfriendly escort

our resident *blue-tongued skink*

who proceeds with a reptilian swagger

     a monitor, lizard, crocodile

perhaps a snake-like slithery swagger

it moves just fast enough
to dissuade its avian not-friends
from comfortably stepping nearer

eventually
with the lizard safely immersed
beneath a pile of rotting compost
the magpie gang

A Blue-Tongued Lizard Life

those back-yard conquering
heroes

resume a strut
around their
gratefully liberated
territory

ideas in the drain

the lizard appears —
as a head
above a grate —
watching the world go by him

it is different up in the air

too much light
after residence in a drain

there is a taste on the breeze
that is not quite enough
but . . .

almost

he'd like to emerge
entire
until the car horn sounds
and a wheel rolls by
too close and too big
and too *much*
for him to understand

in the darkness of the drain
afterwards
there is such a lot to dream
and the taste is still there
like an *idea-trap* that has been set

    [snap]

to inspire him

comprehension of this and of the other

the lizard knows everything
as he looks up
toward the blue

the world is in the brightness
and within the sense he holds
of light

the world
is in the sounds

the lizard strives
to taste the sky

the lizard knows everything
as he looks
into the dark

the world is in the inky night
and in the blackened absence of day
the world is in the echoed bounce
of sound

the lizard understands that black
is plus
or minus
the sky

everything that is all

the lizard
with his tail in his mouth
is everything

the more he takes
the more he is . . .

the more he is
the same

he is the lizard

that is all

the lizard
that is all

so long as

who made the lizard

I wonder
does he wonder

who made the lizard

I wonder
does he care

so long as sun shines

so long as warm
kisses his skin

so long as night ends
in a new sun
does the lizard stop and pause
to wonder

I wonder

alone

the lizard goes out
to where no lizard ever went

hauls a swag
doffs a dangle-corked hat
and
across the broad driveway he roams

until the shade of a fence
as the sun trails the West
and the path through deep shadows
his own

there are adventures to find
on that far other side
until he tires of it all
then
to home

but for now
from his nose down
to the stripes of his tail
he is one

just a lizard
alone

interrogation

the face of God
is a cloud piled high

snow

silver
beneath the grey

the voice is a black
that is rich and deep
with questions
sent into the deep
of the drain
to seek out the lizard

hiding
a-tremble

below

wizard number one

lizard one is such a
long long long

lizard two
is rather short

why can't I see them
standing nose-to-tail
for once
why do they only show up —
each one —
alone

they make me doubt I know
what is going on

was that *lizard two*
or *lizard one*
or
are they
really both the same

first

    over here

they are really the same

    no
    look there
    inside the drainpipe

    then over . . .

A Blue-Tongued Lizard Life

hey
beneath the roll-a-door

and who was it just fell to earth
when I moved that scrap
of sheet iron

lizard one
I'm *sure* it was
but
who can tell

I do believe
in multi-lizards

perhaps by magic

a little hocus
then some pocus
till I'm confused

I think *that* shortness
was *lizard two*
but now
he's gone

Frank Prem

a dude need not seem to move

aauuurrgghh you lizard!

you've fooled me
again

I was searching for you
by the roll-a-door
but then I saw you
looking out the drain

oh slow lizard
how is it that you move
so fast

I know I saw you
where I saw you

I know full well
that you were there

and yet
and yet
I see your head
old lizard
in profile you look sharp

a dude

I guess you move
without looking like you're trying

just appear
where you need to be
and *when* you need to be

A Blue-Tongued Lizard Life

I'm keeping watch dear lizard
I'm going to catch you
between *my* here
and *your*
over there

done well

are you the god
or the daemon

does a lizard *have* a god
inside

a driving hand
that guides you
as you run between the rhythm
and the goals
that are your life

be true to you
follow your lizard heart
to what must be done

done well

and *when* it's done
then may you also die
done well

the masque to soar

when he dons the mask
he is *The Lizard*

scincidaen snout
raised to the air
a walk that is both sway
and saunter

feels his way by the taste
of honeyed sun
head up head up
he is so lizard-proud
so lizard-sure

but in the hole
again
in the empty tunnel
when the dark has closed
is an end to games

there is nothing now
but mask
to claim last certainties
as the long night falls
while shivers seem
so very much . . .

too near

he aches
through hungry hours
for the light of another
holy day

yo ho the rain goes on

well well
ahoy there my shipmates
beware for the water's rising
ahoy
ahoy
here comes the swell

brace yourselves
to ride across the waves
a pirate's life is for the brave
don't cause the roving eye
to light on you

no matter what you do
you'll do darn well
to survive a sail on this briny hell
keeping out of the steely gaze
of Captain Blue

it has been raining for days
raining for nights

the sunny basking afternoons
with snout in the air
soft grasses
and the warmth of baked concrete
have vanished

now the thunder rages
as though bitten
and the lightning plays through the air
like retribution

A Blue-Tongued Lizard Life

down in the drain
the waters first seeped
then crept
then ran
in a noisy rush
of no ending

there is no home here now
for a lizard
save for a stray corner of pine board
broken away
from an old apple crate

a crouch

a shiver

then a curl
into a huddle

as the rain
goes on

yo ho
yo ho
oh what pirates are we
sailing our ship
across a storm-drain sea

lizards shaka-sha

a feather from a magpie

one from a white cockatoo

*the pit from the heart
of a prunus plum*

look
oh look . . .

a rusted nail

*a strand of orange
come away
from a coil baling twine*

*a tarnished silver talisman
that once adorned a young girl's wrist*

there they are
worn around the head
of the lizard shaman

he dances

left legs
right legs
held in the air

shakes his dandelion staff
to release florets
to the sky

A Blue-Tongued Lizard Life

incants
incants

his tail rattles
like a St Vitus snake

    shaka-shaka-sha shaka-sha

bless lizards
everywhere

to see a man

first he stood on four good legs
and waddled as he walked

he raised his head above the grass
to see
all there was to see

he raised his head
up
through the grate
and strained
beyond the drain

he clawed up with his two front legs
to see
all there was to see

he reached up high on the veranda pole
rose above the plants and flowers

stood up tall and nearly straight

like that

to see
all there was to see

walked upright and strolled for hours

stopped to sniff a rose

then gazed
across the green grass wide
to see all
that a man could see

A Blue-Tongued Lizard Life

a way to fly

on the third day of gazing
from the grate
up into the sky
he saw the birds again

resolved
he whispered to a spider

    please

with the gift of web
he spun and wove
gossamer all around himself

the magpie too
left a gift
of black and white
that he ought to include

    done

he scrambled to the height
of a veranda post
clutched the cloth
one corner
for the claws of each
of his four feet

when the breeze rose up
when the sun shone warm
and when the blue that was the sky
made a picture . . .

when he drew his breath
when he'd calmed his thoughts
and when he'd flung himself
to the mercy of air

then
he fell for a while

then
the ground rose close

and then
the grasses luffed near

just underneath him

until
the lizard flew

until
the lizard soared

until the swirl
of a rising current
sustained him

then he turned in air
and looped through a loop

rose
as high in the sky
as the birds

little blues skitter

skitter down baby blue
there's a car running over your drain pipe
and the grate is no place
for you to lose your head
so
skitter right down
baby blue

turn around little blue
your daddy's lazing beneath the garage
and there's no good will come
if you're squished under the sun
so
turn around little blue
turn around

shrine

what is it

how would a lizard know

~

from under the paving stone
where so many slither
to cling
and to die

a shell

the process of extraction —
grip without fracture —
requires gentle firmness
and dexterity

a slow saurian waddle
across grass
and concrete

avoidance of the lightning movement
of a vehicle coming to halt
in the carport

then a subtle twitch
and pivot
to enter the grating
into the storm-water pipe

back in the deeper darkness again
it is a delicate process
to raise above the earlier arrangements
and place this trophy

A Blue-Tongued Lizard Life

number twenty eight

at the apex of the triangle
backed against the canyon wall
of the drain

~

a lizard cannot know
but there is a symmetry
a comforting air and feeling

encouragement enough
to start another

love of the sun

the lizard raised
his head from the ground
to reach toward the sky
and the sun

blinked

so sweet
was the warm pouring down
he wished he could take it below

for the den where he lives
at the end of the drain
is cosy but so empty
in darkness

he wished he could hold
the sun within his claw
to carry as his beacon

>*oh sun*

he cried

>*I am in love with your light*
>*I long*
>*to lie down*
>*in your warm*
>
>*come with me*
>*let me show you my den*

A Blue-Tongued Lizard Life

*let us banish the dark with your light
with you I'll be charmed
and your warm will be
my balm*

*come with me
down below
come with me down
below*

the sun will not
entertain a lizard's court
though it is a flattering thing
to be adored

a single beam
for the lizard lover
is all the sun
would give forth

lizard
caught it within a claw
and he took it to his home

now he sleeps
through the night
and he is warm

the skink who loved the sun
sleeps warm

sleep in the dark of the moon

he climbed up
on the star-way stair
up
until he reached the moon

licked both lips
with his broad blue tongue
and ate her
right out of the sky

in the dark
replete
he curled himself around
tail to nose
as he fell into sleep

it was then he saw
that moon
so fair
return as a sliver
and a shining light
that grew
and grew

until at the full
he awoke at last
from his dream

in the deep of the drain
just a strange

so pretty

small dream

smiling home

the smile of the lizard
is a trick of the light
for the face of a lizard
is stone

as the day hurries past
between shadow and bright
full relief is a lizard
alone

but when night falls hard
and the dark descends
the shape that is *lizard*
is gone

the lizard himself
both willow and wisp
in a blink of the light
has turned home

the lizard himself
is home

reflection

the progress is slow
even for this cautious one

he approaches

stops

bobs his head low

peers forward

wary
looks to each side

behind

weaves forward

opens a wide yawn and
his-s-s-s
fierce and sharp

silence hisses in return

>*a step forward*
>*nose*
>*to nose*
>
>*tongue out*
>*tongue out*

a handsome contemplation

>*move left*
>*move right*

A Blue-Tongued Lizard Life

admirable stripes

> *raises his head*
> *raises his head*

a sleek tail

> *slow blink*
> *slow blink*

a turn away
. . .

the reflection
is gone
merely a tail
merging into distance

breakfast dance

taking my lizard
for a walk on a lead
doffing our hats
to each person we see

into a café
where I hold the door
for my lizard who enters
with a crawl 'cross the floor

and I'll have a 'cino
the lizard
a snail
we're out to be seen
oh
we're both wearing *Tails*

dance between tables
the lizard and I
a tango
a quick step
raw egg and hot pie

then down at the table
breathless

and laughing

and foolish

and high

we waltz through the morning
the lizard and I

Lizzie Blue steps out (1)

Lizzie Blue has primped her stripes
dabbed colour on her tongue

she's walking out on the concrete curb
under the midday sun

switches her tail
in a r-r-r-roiling roll

blinks her eyes
in a *come-along* call

Lizzie Blue
has primped all of her stripes
and the colour
is on
her
tongue

Lizzie Blue steps out (2)

Elspeth Indigo
primps up each scale
works the taste of dark stripes
into her shingles

dabs the end of her tongue
in a wild
violent gentian
fade-edged away
into pink
upon purple

then out of the drain
to display
on the plinth
a languor that's laced up
in longing

she shines in the sun
like a mirror-caught light
she shines
as brilliant as diamond

water for the little bandit

I'm wheeling round the veranda
I see a bandit in a Zorro mask
hiding below my fridge

whoa-ho

I'll play you little bandit
put a spot of treasure
just a little way out of your reach

what you going to do
I see your nose appearing

what you going to do
I've been watching half an hour

what you going to do
just raise your claw
then put it back down

what you going to do
at last
I can almost see your tail

it's been nearly one hour

you are slow mister bandit
you are taking much too long
with your leg up in the air
then your leg back on the ground

head up
like a sphinx you stand but

stop

freeze for just a moment
and *stop*
could that have been a sound
and *stop*

stop

it is such a lot of work you do
for a little drop of juice
such a round-a-bout-a-way
to getting what you want

no
I can't take this longer

no
I just have to move

no
no
I've been watching
way too long so go on go on
go on and get back under
your bandit hiding bar fridge
I'm not watching you anymore

I'm not watching you
I'm not watching you
no I'm not watching you
at all

(I see you there)

the advanced hatchlings

dom dom *dom-da-dom-dom-dom*	*bwa bwa bwa* *bwa-ba-bwa-ba-bwa*
dom dom *dom-da-dom-dom-dom*	*b-waaaaaaa bwa* *bwa-ba-bwa-ba-bwa*
pork pie hat dark black glasses	coo-ool baby just cool
dom dom *dom-da-dom-dom-dom*	*bwa bwa bwa* *bwa-ba-bwa-ba-bwa*
dom dom *dom-da-dom-dom-dom*	*b-waaaaaaa bwa* *bwa-ba-bwa-ba-bwa*
white cuffs black links trumpet on a tie	derby hat tuxedo vest two-toned shoes
dom dom *dom-da-dom-dom-dom*	*bwa bwa bwa* *bwa-ba-bwa-ba-bwa*
dom dom *dom-da-dom-dom-dom*	*b-waaaaaaa bwa* *bwa-ba-bwa-ba-bwa*
hi hi well hi hi hi hi	hey hey hey hey hey

dom dom
dom-da-dom-dom-dom

dom dom

b-waaaaaaa
bwa bwa bwa
bwa-ba-bwa-ba-bwa-wa

horn to his lips
sweet sweet licks

a-live
this lizard's a-live
yeh

bwa-bwa-ba

dom dom
dom-da-dom-dom-dom

bwa bwa bwa
bwa-ba-bwa-ba-bwa

b-waaaaaaa bwa

ta tinka tink
ta-tinka-tinka-tinka
reee-yuuu-reee-yuuu-reee

black key white key
every note tonight key

a-live
this skink's
yeh a-live

dom dom
bwa-bwa-bwa-da
reee-yuuu-reee-yuuu
ta-tink-a-tink bwa-bwa

yeh

spoor

it could be the silver lines
of a snail
gliding across the contour
of the garden

a trail that can be followed
with the eyes

or the staling mess
of gravy meat
that hasn't been wholly eaten
by the dog

a scent that kisses soul
through a trembling tongue

it could be the hurried need
to find a mate
that rises in the heat
of Summer

with an itch that can make a *Rex*
of a timid *Saur*

it could be a persistent idea
of the warm dark
that turns a skink around
to a different path

with a feeling that holds the power
of a search for home

perhaps it's just
a kind of slow beating
from the deep down
of a reptile's heart

and a prevailing sense
of true belonging
that is enough to keep the lizard
whole

A Blue-Tongued Lizard Life

on the move with Zorro

Zorro
the young blue
is on the move

slow swimming
through the long grass

tongue whipping the air
to test for safety
he has snuck around
a corner

sidled beside a wall
to hide
behind a handy gumboot
there to test the air
again

then he's away
sedately lizard waddle

away away
to parts that we
don't yet know

around another corner

towards a fence
that catches sunlight

a concrete plinth to bake
on
with a safety nook
just below

Zorro
is on the move today

perhaps tomorrow
I will see him

over

.

.

.

there

.

.

.

over there

or even

over *there*

I will see him
but I don't know

More Lizards

four elemental uses for light

1.

in the dark of the den
he sings the light
to show the bones
of his home

gapes his mouth wide
a silent sound
that slowly brightens the hole

a sharpened claw
on the green-brown wall
is the mark
of a life below

etching done
light released
curled round
back into the dream

Frank Prem

the lizard on Main Street

through the magic
of a snail shell
that has twirled in
on itself
the lizard strives
until he turns into
a man

his legs elongate
like a pair of poles

his tail becomes
much less

front legs extend into arms
and each claw
is just right for a manicure

and a polish

shoulders
fill out a jacket
chest inside a shirt
he strides in trousers
that are the latest blue jeans

what's wrong with that . . .

well nothing

he is sartorial
as anything
at the Stock Exchange
but

More Lizards

sadly
it's true

his head still belongs
to a lizard
even though he's six foot
three

he is
a lizard on legs and while
mostly
he fits right in on Main Street
a lizard in a suit
still seems
out of place

first crack of morning

in the land
that was always darkness
and night time

colour waves lay
a little
here

some over there

the lizard set himself
to plait
a mighty sound

gleam by gleam
he claimed each strand
to twist together

ray on ray
a length of light
braided into thong

and then the darkness
of his home
was black complete

save for one tight coil
of shimmer
in the corner

it was done

he looped around
that bullwhip

More Lizards

then he swirled and swirled
the lash

roaring through the air

and snapped it **[C-RACK]**

the shout of morning

snapped again **[C-RACK]**

to end the night

snapped **[C-RACK]**
snapped **[C-RACK]**
snapped [**C-RACK**]

to start the sun
to rise

the new gecko

the marbled geckos
have come to stay

I've seen one
far away up the back
of the block
where the wood rounds
lie waiting for the axe
and me

and I've seen another
here
close by the house
so I guess this is home
now
it seems the geckos
would like to stay

liz-again

the big blue-tongue
is in the drainpipe

the big bluey
has returned

he looks twice the liz
he once was

do all of them grow
in their sleep

it's been a long
and wet winter

all the lizards
buried themselves deep

but now the sun
has warmed the ether

and the drainpipe
is full of lizards

once again

prince little blue

shine shine little blue
sunlight
bright your scales

slow blink

the day
is passing

your daddy owns
the drain
mama
is in the woodpile

shine bright
little blue
warm now
are your dark stripes

you prince
of broken bricks
bake now
upon their ridgelines

a rubble mountain
to recline upon with pride
here
could be your domain

shine bright
small blue

shine shine

More Lizards

the unsuccessful journey of lizards to the promised land

all right all right

the leader said

*all those of you
who do not know
the way
make a line*

make a line there

make a line

*come up close
come up close*

come up closer

*take a tail
in your mouth
but do not bite it*

*I said
a tail in your mouth
but no
no biting*

*now first rank
you may proceed*

*second rank
you may proceed*

third rank
oh no
who dropped their tail

fourth rank
oh no
oh no oh no

in the chaos
of half the lizards
seeking their tails
running over everybody else's

and the wriggling
un-control
of detached
and discarded rears

the leader —
when out of the assembly's gaze —
slipped beneath
a convenient boulder
curled up his own nose
to his own tail

and waited

Way Poems

with your assistance

goodnight mama
I'm going to walk that way

bye bye my papa
I've got to walk that way

onto the path that is waiting
I am ready to walk that way

don't cry
don't miss me
we have all got to walk
that way

and I have seen you
this one time
now
I can walk that way

will you help me

will you hold
my hand

will you stay awake at my side
while I am sleeping
while I am walking
when I am leaving

when I go

help me
help me to walk
that way

who knew the way

he caught the cloud
that flew too low
turned it around
and sent it out that way

he paused the wind
by holding his hands
before his eyes
then reached out
to turn it aside that way

he bent down low
his face nearly
into the pond
smoothed each wrinkle
with a hand
that swept away

the fish and he
knew the flow undisturbed
though tempest raged
and that nothing need tremble
when it knew the way

to a higher place

>boil
>you slow-to-bubble philistine
>whey-face
>of wasted time

he is talking to
at
the milk
poured into a saucepan
on the stovetop

>the brown grumbler
>is roaring it's head off at me
>and you
>you
>are not even trying

>haste
>or I'll tip you out
>and start over

he doesn't mean that
not really

but judging the sweet timing
that brings coffee
to percolation
at the same moment
as milk to the boil
is art rather than science

and his agitation to achieve
precision
itself boils over into impatience
when he has to wait on one element
or the other

> *there*
>
> *there you are*

crooning now

bubbles bubbles
the surface over

bubbles

> *now I can quick you*
> *to the cup*

the coffee is still complaining
a slightly slower scowl
in the percolator

nothing has been lost

the flavour
bitter . . .

sweet

who knows
perhaps his routine
of distress and irritability
had a supportive effect

ahhh

regardless
it is his way
to the higher place
and every day
he gets there

the poet

in the morning
while she gazed through glass

> *the play of light*
>
> *the sway of trees*
> *in new dressed green*
>
> *(it is springtime*
> *after all)*
>
> *dapples spread across grass*
> *where the two merged*
>
> *lovers*
> *at the height of their season*

restlessness grew
a feeling inside
of tightness

angsty

in the afternoon
almost beside herself
with pent agitation
she gave herself the push

that urged her

> *be*
> *still*

to let the tensions flow
into thought

    her mother

thick wool
where thoughts should live

    her father

one gasp
and that may be all

    the garden

what if the seeds take root
today

where is the trail
that leads through
this winding

which word
to start
this on its way

and then . . .

and there . . .

the poem is done
the mood is light
the evening calls
with a smile
sublime

another leg
of her journey
is over
another mood that drove her
fulfilled

another thought
is contained in amber

all in all
it has been another day

all in all
another day
well done

the five steps to wheaten pecks

the old man progresses
five steps at a time
to reach a wall
a fence
that he can lean on

air that tastes
so sweet
is hard these days
to come by

a moment of rest
until the *gasps* calm down
to *breathing*
then

five steps more

and five steps more
again

it is important to keep moving
even though the atmosphere
is so thin
down here on planet earth
for
the hen —
the last remaining hen —
is waiting

she has no flock
to be part of
they have passed away
one by one
to a cat
to a fox
to a feather-depleting
old age

and now she waits
for the shuffle
of him
beside the yard gate

in her nest
is an egg

he sits down
beside the laying box
on a chair he positioned there
some time ago

in his hand
a covered palm
of golden wheat

she dainty-steps
until she can stand
upon him —
on his knees —
to take each grain

one peck

one peck at a time
until they're gone

and then she leaves him
goes off
to forage in the yard
again

and he
can take his five steps
all the way back
to the rest
of his life

perhaps by questions

he stood at the end
of the concrete path
just below
the washing line

raised his head
and shouted out
into the blue
his name

>*I am . . .*

>*I am . . .*

he yelled it at the sky

shouted through
the clouds
into beyond
and then a little bit further

a little bit more

his name came back
reflected in the sunlight
diffused among the new green
leaves of the trees

his name came back
magnified
by the action of light
diffuse daylight

> *who*
> *do you think you are*

profound
deep question

> *who do you think*
> *you are*

he fell down to his knees

> *I don't know*
>
> *I don't know I don't know*
>
> *I am just a question*
> *I have asked answer of the breeze*
>
> *do you know*
>
> *do you know*

but the breeze has gone
and the day is done
and the light fades dark
and the sun bids goodbye
and tomorrow beckons
with answers
to the

> *why*
>
> *why*
> *I don't know*
> *but my task lies*
> *in questions*

and I will ask the sun
I will ask the stars

I will ask . . .

perhaps forever
I will ask

three birds

the black swan has no legs
majesty alone propels her
prow and wake

serenity

she crosses water

~

the pelican has no legs
his flight of wings
are caught by wind
whose joy it is
to hold him high
in the air

~

the gannet has no legs
before the bullet of her mind
the waves
with grace bid welcome

embrace her
like a daughter

journey by boat

mother night
I have grown weary
for the sea of this sky is long
and I have crossed her
one end to another
above the earth I've blown

my sun-boat that glowed golden
is leading me
towards home

mother night
come take me
to your arms where I may rest
for I have steered the ship of day
across heaven

my sun-boat has shone —
beacon to the shoal —
and westward now I am returning
my boat
knows
where it must go

poor saturations

how much oxygen
in your fingers?

> *one hundred per cent sat*
> *ninety-five*

how your lungs must work so
when you love your cigarette

do you know
that this is dying

I wonder
do you care

light another cigarette
old friend of mine
old fool

~

how much oxygen
in your fingers?

> *eighty-eight percent sat*
> *eighty-three*

feel the world start closing in
but still
another cigarette
will help to clear your head

let me light you up
old idiot old good friend
I can see you are dying
anyway

~

how much oxygen
in your fingers?

>*sixty-five percent sat*
>*down to thirty-eight*

and you don't feel much like cigarettes
when there's an ambulance
in your doorway
to put the mask across your face

try to breathe
while the machine's still yelping

breathe
for life is all there is
dear boy

~

how much dioxide
in your fingers?

I fear
there is no room
there is no room
for
anymore

a court farewells its king

when the tomb was bared
the king
appeared to be at rest

his face towards home
his hands held
in peaceful pose

the queen . . .

she was beside him
in a separate space
she too was serene
as though no more
than sleeping

a maid had twisted
from her side
to gaze up
skywards

the cousin seemed to feel
the lack of air
clutching at her throat
to aid
one more shallow breath

the harem in disorder
hands holding tears
to long lost eyes

the weakest one
had crawled
beneath her last bed
to hide

the eunuch from the gates
on guard
here
for eternity
has parted from his head

all covered over in an hour
two thousand years ago

just
as it was meant
to be

how I thought, it was

I thought it
with my heart
so I could say it
with my tongue
so I could see it
with my eyes
so I could hear it
with my ears
so I could breathe it
through my nose

and what I said
it was
and what I saw
it was
and what I heard
it was
and what I smelt
it was

I could *feel* it

so I reported
to my head
and it reported
right back to my heart

and so it was
from nothing

that
is what I thought

barrow and spade

wheelbarrow waits
impatiently

it is parked
in the middle of the yard

the spade is at rest
and idly bides its time

they waited for me all day
yesterday
but I
was otherwise delayed
earning
not shovelling
sometimes that seems to be
the way

but now
I hear the compost call
the mulch has grown
in its demands

so
load and fill the barrow
move the muck from the trailer tray
mix mulch and horse-potatoes
in a mound
that will be tomorrow's garden

now watch the hot steam rise —
a smoke —
wafting from the venting pipe
that's good heat in there
so
keep your hand away

the wheelbarrow waits —
more patient now —
it leans
against the garden shed wall

the spade is at rest
nonchalant
could be its name

but it will be ready
when the call to mould
the garden earth
happens
once again
to come its way

sorrow and joy (up here in heaven)

oh moon
you must leave me
here in heaven

I will wreath myself
in cloud
to hide my weeping

and yet
my moon
when you are gone
up here in heaven I
will shine
in high delight

for though you must leave
faded to nothing
away
and beyond my touch

it is only a shadow

it is only my shadow
and that too will pass

while I
impatient
await you

up here
in heaven

conversation with three foxes

ha-aarr

ha-aarr

the sleek black crow landed lightly
and opened proceedings
with mild humour

a very light touch
for the corvidae kind

~

easy for you to laugh

the first fox spoke

I still believe
I'd be innocent
before a jury

one paltry chicken
yes
I managed to get home
where the den is always hollow

but the attempt at lamb
that they did me for
well
that was no more
than my true nature

who am I
if I
am not me

~

and I

spoke up another

what of me

I ate nothing that night
I had just begun
stopped the once
to sniff the air
for danger

yes
you can laugh at that
it costs you nil

and even for me
there is no charge now
my account
is square
beyond remainders
or residues

~

      ha-aarr

      ha-aarr

the corvid
still attentive

~

      yarp
      yarp

shrilled into the wind

      yarp
      yarp

she has no scope
for conversation

her mind is gone
the wind
sighs through it

      yarp
      yarp

to the quarters
her voice
is thrown

~

enough

barked the first

> *I have spoken*
> *all I can of this*
>
> *enough*
> *I've other places*
> *to go*
>
> *other places I should see*

and the kind crow concurred
with a peck —
delicately gentle —
to pluck the last
un-shining orb

a spread of silk and jet
strong wings
and a circled laugh

> *ha-aarr*

three foxes were bid
goodbye

I creator

the brush
that touched the page
was a miracle

from blank emptiness
into hues that started life
for a picture of the world
spun blue and white

suspended in jet

littered with sparkles
and pinpoints

who knows
what the artist
of that world has done

> *on the land*
> *down in the oceans*
> *high up above*
> *deep into the sky*

another page
another pen
another colour
and
another closure of the eyes
to peer within

there

Frank Prem

another palette
that holds every colour
I
could ever need

open to new

it's a new world
every time
I open my eyes

because I

> *had a new thought*

> *looked in a new place*

> *was surprised by an idea*

> *noticed the dust swirl*
> *under the sunlight*

> *was profound-ed*
> *by my joy*

it's a new world
every time my eyes
close

because I
see the pattern of the lamp's light
play across my eyelid
watch as all the dark spots
move

drift away in an idea
boat on a thought sea
pulse and pulse and pulse
my blood flow

feel my heart rate rise
when I think of you
and me
in a wide new world

it's a brand
brand
brand new world

every thing that I see
every time that I think
every blink when I close my
eyes are open
to new worlds

boat to the island

boat
the current calls

will you carry me

unfurl your sail
then let us drift together
beneath the sun

the lazy breeze
knows me well
and to where I'm bound

~

boat
raise a little wake
for me

that I might feel the salt
and spray
as though we sail
for pleasure

my friend the breeze
has riffled my shirt
and you
are steadfast

~

boat
let's circle once
around the island

the surf
broken on a shoal

the harbour

then tell the breeze
that I am ready
to ride the current
and her sweet luff
home

in anger

I spoke to the sky

    ANGER

is what I called

    ANGER

I shouted out
from my heart

in every inflection
I placed my rage

stamped my feet
hard
upon the ground

waved
both my fists
at the air
clenched
as tight as I
can clench them

    OH OH
    OH
    how I am ANGRY

I am so angry

hear me placid sky

is what I raged

~

in the corner of the sky
grew one grey tendril

curled upon itself
it boiled
in a small way

and grew

it writhed

it made a cloud

grey grey
grew into the sky
placid no more

it growled
grumbled

lightning flashed
from out of the storm
that roared now
and rumbled

even the stars had fled
even the moon

only the sun stood

as black as the bright

the sun shone
darkness

~

I
I stood beneath a storm
afraid of the lightning
afraid of the roar
unable to stand

I . . .

I looked at the storm
and I
felt —
gradually —
a fear flow my way
projected by thunder
illumined by lightning

and I knew
the thing I had done

After Words

Index of Poems

A

above and below 29
a court farewells its king 263
a day with the dog 61
a dude need not seem to move 200
a fall of finches 16
allowed 185
alone 196
amaze me 76
anchor 31
angling the big deep 20
an uncertainty in silver 19
an unseen presence - I waiting - the wren 177
a semblance that remains 160
a silky leap of starlings 131
a sketch of the season 159
a study in meteorology 11
a sun-burnt trilling 48
at Fyan's Creek 182
at Koko Black 92
author, author 17
autumn leaving 136
a way to fly 209

B

barefoot 138
barrow and spade 266
be-bop night 112
boat to the island 277
breakfast dance 220

C

calling out salt 146
cockatoo committee 43
comprehension of this and of the other 193
conquering heroes 189
conversation with three foxes 269

currawong sky 58

D

done well 202

E

eagle 56
eejit magpie 137
elementals 151
everything that is all 194

F

fetching the firewood 164
first crack of morning 236
first salt 90
flashing 103
flash mob in Deniliquin 118
for my help 33
four elemental uses for light 233
free-verse song 179

G

gnarly country 176
god of the mountain 173
golden slumber 82
goodnight moonlight 75
gravity 158

H

harlequin blue-tongue 125
harsh laughter 52
have you listened 84
hot 130
how I thought, it was 265
huff the lights out 51
hungry dog 73
huntsman (three strikes) 68
hush 83
hush, there's a bear . . . 119

I

I creator 273
ideas in the drain 192
in anger 279
in circles 8
in Daylesford, the news 123
indigo u 7
in six small stanzas 168
interrogation 197
in the path of a fire 133
into sleep 129

J

journey by boat 260

K

keyed all alone 149

L

lament for a lost _uzz (1) 22
lament for a lost _uzz (2) 23
laughing 166
little blues skitter 211
liz-again 239
lizards shaka-sha 206
Lizzie Blue steps out (1) 221
Lizzie Blue steps out (2) 222
love of the sun 214
lunching at The Kookaburra Hotel 180

M

marsupials, maternals, matriarchs 175
meeting Nola 121
mind so 5
Mister Frank - simply the best 147
modestly (begun) 101
moon and light 70
mopoke 32
my girl (the mantis) 41

N

Ned's Bakery (Beechworth) 21

O

observations 184
old traffic stoppers 99
on the move with Zorro 229
open to new 275

P

perhaps by questions 256
poor saturations 261
porch or veranda 107
prince little blue 240
prrrty 24

R

rain catching 78
rain-song 46
reflection 218
remove my hat 104

S

self portrait via life-draw 161
shadow 9
shadow dancing 59
shaman 132
sharp 15
shrine 212
six ways to measure time (on a visit to the big smoke) 86
sky rupture 47
sleep in the dark of the moon 216
small, like yesterday 183
smiling home 217
sniffing the cusp of Spring 174
so long as 195
song of a road 88
sorrow and joy (up here in heaven) 268
space debris 140
spoor 227

Spring sound 109
stab and howl 117
state of min . . . (gee-up) 35
step inside fourteen 142
still - rising 115
stitch winter 144
sweet and slow 81
sweet dream 37

T

that hare o' mine 181
the advanced hatchlings 225
the blackberry 55
the concept of . . . 6
the doggy in the morning 72
the escaping 95
the five steps to wheaten pecks 253
the girl who had her red shoes on 45
the last mellow 53
the lizard on Main Street 234
the locale 10
the masque to soar 203
the new gecko 238
the old lady's parrot 153
the poem insomnia 105
the poet 250
there again (the corri-dog) 25
the solo dancer attempts an explanation 79
the terrible malady of Miss Shirl 157
the tree is to bird is to tree is to 108
the unsuccessful journey of lizards to the promised land 241
the wooing of the wind 54
three birds 259
three echoes 13
to a higher place 247
to breathe 85
to defy 114
to love you is . . . 116
to my mind 34
to see a man 208
truck canyon alarm clock (good morning) 163

two insect asides 30
two Kookaburras 100

U

uke-latin (olé) 26
ukulele nights 167
unless . . . 145

V

very local knowledge 49

W

Wangaratta tandem 110
washing a day 96
water for the little bandit 223
wattle and heart 27
when flying 12
who is the girl? 65
who knew the way 246
wild 67
wind song 71
with your assistance 245
wizard number one 198

Y

yo ho the rain goes on 204

Author Information

Frank Prem has been a storytelling poet since his teenage years. He has been a psychiatric nurse through all of his professional career, which now exceeds forty years.

He has been published in magazines, online zines, and anthologies in Australia, and in a number of other countries, and has both performed and recorded his work as spoken word.

Frank is an Adjunct Research Associate of the School of Education, Charles Sturt University, Australia.

He lives with his wife in the beautiful township of Beechworth in North East Victoria, Australia.

Connect with Frank

Find Frank at his website www.FrankPrem.com, or through Social Media online at Facebook, X (Twitter), Instagram and YouTube.

Other Published Works

Free Verse Poetry

Small Town Kid (2018)
Devil In The Wind (2019)
The New Asylum (2019)
Herja, Devastation - With Cage Dunn (2019)
Walk Away Silver Heart (2020)
A Kiss for the Worthy (2020)
Rescue and Redemption (2020)
Pebbles to Poems (2020)
The Garden Black (2022)
A Specialist at The Recycled Heart (2022)
Ida: Searching for The Jazz Baby (2023)
From Volyn to Kherson (2023)
Alive Is What You Feel (2023)
White Whale (2024)
Small Change (2025)

A Poetry Archive

A Poetry Archive Volume 1 (2024)
A Poetry Archive Volume 2 (2024)
A Poetry Archive Volume 3 (2024)
A Poetry Archive Volume 4 (2024)
A Poetry Archive Volume 5 (2025)

Bachelard Interpreted

A Choir of Whispers: Bachelard Interpreted book 1 (2024)
A Cleansing Flame: Bachelard Interpreted book 2 (2024)
Real Weight: Bachelard Interpreted book 3 (2025)
A Flight of Ideas: Bachelard Interpreted book 4 (2025)

Picture Poetry/Spoken Image

Voices (In The Trash) (2020)
The Beechworth Bakery Bears (2021)
Sheep On The Somme (2021)
Waiting For Frank-Bear (2021)
A Lake Sambell Walk (2021)
A Few Places Near Home (2023)
The Cielonaut (2024)
Pilgrim Volume 1 - Illustrated by Leanne Murphy (2024)

Wild Arancini Classics

Alice's Adventures In Wonderland (illustrated edition) by Lewis Carroll
Heidi (illustrated edition) by Joanna Spyri
The Man From Snowy River And Other Verses by A. B. (The Banjo) Patterson
On Our Selection (illustrated edition) by Steele Rudd
Treasure Island (illustrated edition) by R. L. Stevenson
Japanese Fairy Tales (illustrated edition) by Y. T. Ozaki
Russian Fairy Tales by W. R. S. Ralston
The Adventures of Sherlock Holmes (illustrated edition) by Arthur Conan Doyle

What Readers Say

Small Town Kid

A modern-day minstrel. Highly recommended.
—A. F. (Australia)

Small Town Kid is a wonderful collection.
—S. T. (Australia)

Devil In The Wind

Trust me, this book will stay with you. Bravo!
—K. K. (USA)

Moving, beautiful, and terrible. I was left with a profound sense of respect, as well as a reminder that we should never take for granted every precious every moment of life.
—J. S. (South Africa)

The New Asylum

Words can't do justice to the emotional journey I travelled in (reading this collection).
—C. D. (Australia)

If I had to pick one book over the past year that has truly resonated with me, this would be it.
—K. B. (USA)

Walk Away Silver Heart

Instantly grips you by the throat in his step-by-step story of survival. Bravo!
—K. K. (USA)

Outstanding!
—B. T. (Australia)

A Kiss For The Worthy

A Celebration of Life Written in Thoughtful Bursts of Poetic Expression
—C M C (United States)

With every verse, I found myself reflecting about myself, my life, and the world.
—K

Rescue and Redemption

The passion of love in its many forms explored by one for another.
—J L (United States)

I've enjoyed every word, every breath. Every moment within the life of these stories.
—C D (Australia)

Sheep On The Somme

Museums and archivists take note~sell this in your gift shops, preserve it in your archives. Professors, teachers~share with your students.
—A R C (United States)

(This) book is a beautiful and graphic tribute to all those brave men and women who gave their lives for their countries between 1914 and 1918.
—R C (South Africa)

Ida: Searching for The Jazz Baby

I found myself deeply moved by the presentation of Ida's elusive, illusionary life.
—E G (United States)

He gives her a depth and vulnerability that the press didn't.
— A C (United Kingdom

The Garden Black

Prem creates verse that illuminates our world, its experiences and history.
—S C (United Kingdom)

Prem's poetry reminds that life is fragile and fleeting ... both harsh and beautiful.
—D G K (Canada)

A Few Places Near Home

The author has captured many beautiful images in this book, and is a wonderful photographer as well as a poet. This book would make a beautiful coffee table book filled with moving prose to make us ponder with gorgeous accompanying images.
—D K (Canada)

www.FrankPrem.com